CONTENTS

THE MIDDLE JURASSIC

The Middle Jurassic lasted from around 175 to 165 million years ago. The major landmass known as Pangea began to separate into Laurasia and Gondwana, and the Atlantic Ocean began to form as sea levels gradually rose. The arid conditions of the Upper Triassic and Lower Jurassic period gave way to a more humid climate, especially at higher altitude. This encouraged the growth of jungles and forests. While conifers were dominant in the Middle Jurassic, other plants, such as ginkgoes, cycads and ferns, were also major food sources for the plant eaters.

Ocean life flourished during this time as **plesiosaurs** became common and the top marine predators, **pliosaurs**, grew to the size of small whales. New types of dinosaurs such as the **sauropod cetiosaurs** and **brachiosaurs** appeared, as well as the meat-eating **megalosaurs**. In the air, flying reptiles called **pterosaurs** thrived, while small mammals continued to survive and avoid the jaws of **ornithopods**.

D[...]RS
OF T[...] [...]ASSIC

FIREFLY BOOKS

A FIREFLY BOOK

Published by Firefly Books Ltd. 2016

First printing

Publisher Cataloging-in-Publication Data (U.S.)

Names: West, David, 1956-, author.
Title: Dinosaurs of the Middle Jurassic : 25 dinosaurs / David West.
Description: Richmond Hill, Ontario, Canada : Firefly Books, 2016. | Series: Dinosaurs. | Includes index. | Summary: "An illustrated guide of 25 of the best-known dinosaurs of the period, providing up-to-date information with highly detailed computer generated artwork. Illustrated introductory spreads provide background information on the time periods in which the dinosaurs lived" -- Provided by publisher.
Identifiers: ISBN 978-1-77085-835-0 (paperback) | 978-1-77085-836-7 (hardcover)
Subjects: LCSH: Dinosaurs – Juvenile literature.
Classification: LCC QE861.5W478 |DDC 567.9 – dc23

Library and Archives Canada Cataloguing in Publication

West, David, 1956-, author
        Dinosaurs of the middle Jurassic : 25 dinos... / David West.
(Dinosaurs)
Includes index.
ISBN 978-1-77085-836-7 (hardback).--ISBN 978-1-77085-835-0 (paperback)
        1. Dinosaurs--Juvenile literature. 2. Paleontology--Jurassic--Juvenile literature. I. Title.
  QE861.5.W4692 2016   j567.9   C2016-902143-2

Published in the United States by
Firefly Books (U.S.) Inc.
P.O. Box 1338, Ellicott Station
Buffalo, New York 14205

Published in Canada by
Firefly Books Ltd.
50 Staples Avenue, Unit 1
Richmond Hill, Ontario L4B 0A7

Printed in China

Text by David and Oliver West
Illustrations by David West

Produced by David West
Children's Books,
6 Princeton Court, 55 Felsham
Road, London SW15 1AZ

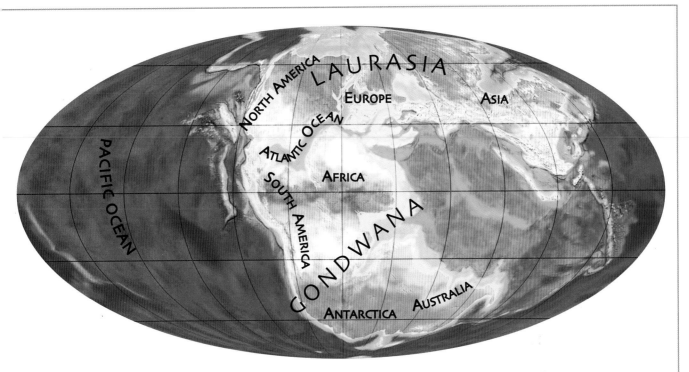

The map above show s the Earth at the time of the Middle Jurassic period 170 million years ago. Below, a scene from China 165 million years ago, shows a Spinophorosaurus (1) defending itself from two Monolophosauruses (2) as a Huayangosaurus (3) runs from the scene. In the distance a group of Omeisauruses (4) arrive at a watering hole.

AGILISAURUS

Agilisaurus means "agile lizard." Its shins were longer than its thigh bones, which is ideal for fast sprinters. This, coupled with its long tail, would have made it an exceptionally agile and speedy little herbivore! *Agilisaurus* was a small **ornithischia**, similar to **ornithopods**. It had a short skull that ended in a beak, which would have been used for raking vegetation off low-lying shrubbery. It also had canines and chisel-like teeth that suggest it fed, too, on small animals such as mammals and lizards.

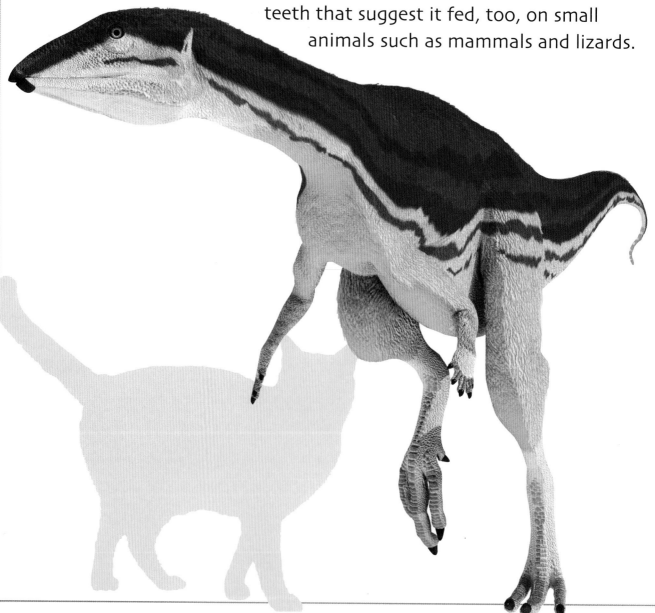

Agilisaurus lived between **170–160 million years ago**. Its fossil remains were found in China, Asia. It grew to a size of approximately 4.9 feet (1.5 m) long and weighed about 75 to 100 pounds (34–45.4 kg).

AMYGDALODON

Amygdalodon was named "almond tooth" because of the shape of its teeth. It was a herbivorous, primitive **sauropod**. It is only known from three specimens, and all of them were very fragmentary partial remains. Scientists think it was quite a long **sauropod** with a typically lengthy neck. This allowed it to browse for vegetation higher up than other herbivores.

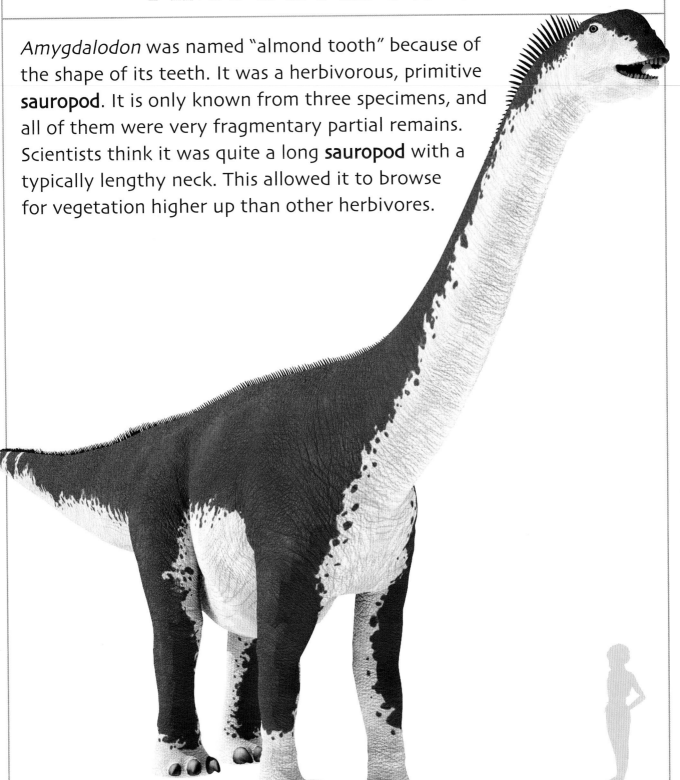

Amygdalodon lived between **177–169 million years ago**. Fossil remains were found in Argentina, South America. It grew to 49.2 feet (15 m) long and weighed more than 22 tons (20 tonnes).

ATLASAURUS

Atlasaurus is named after the Moroccan Atlas Mountains where it was found. In Greek mythology the Titan, Atlas, held up the heavens with his back at the top of these mountains. *Atlasaurus* was a medium to large herbivorous **sauropod** with spatula-shaped teeth for chomping leaves from tall conifers. It had a similar sloping back to *Brachiosaurus*. Its head was large and its neck was quite short. It had a long tail and elongated legs with the forelimbs much longer than the rear ones. It is one of the most complete specimens of a **sauropod** ever found, with an almost entire skeleton that includes part of the skull, which is very rare.

Atlasaurus lived about **165 million years ago**. Fossil remains were found in Morocco, North Africa. It grew to a length of 50 feet (15.2 m) and weighed in the region of 25 tons (22.5 tonnes).

BELLUSAURUS

Bellusaurus means "beautiful lizard." It was a short-necked **sauropod**. It is known from a set of 17 specimens that were found in the same area. All of them were juvenile. It is suspected that a flash flood swept them away, but it is also possible that they tried to cross a river during a migration, but were too small to withstand the current and so were dragged off their feet and drowned.

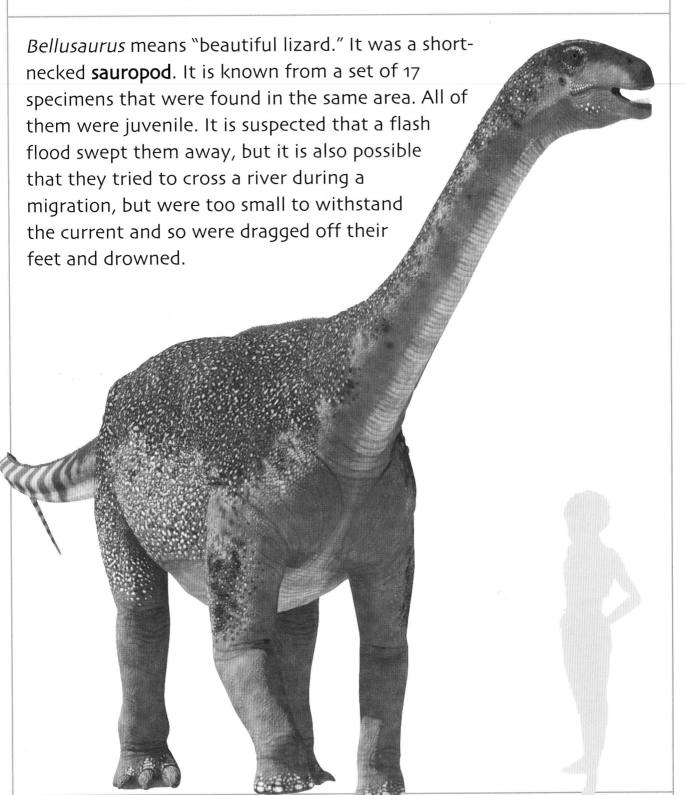

Bellusaurus lived **180–160 million years ago**. Its fossil remains were found in China, Asia. The juvenile specimens were 16 feet (4.9 m) long and weighed around 0.5 tons (0.45 tonnes).

CETIOSAURUS

Cetiosaurus means "whale lizard." The paleontologist who discovered it thought it was a very large crocodile or whale-like creature! It was later correctly identified as a medium-sized herbivorous **sauropod**. It was very large for its time, similar in size to *Diplodocus* and *Apatosaurus*. *Cetiosaurus* was a primitive **sauropod**, its bones were very thick and heavy and, unlike other **sauropods**, they were not hollow. It had a very long neck and a small head, with a robust torso and long, column-like legs.

Cetiosaurus lived **167 million years ago**. Fossil remains were found in England and Western Europe. It grew to 52 feet (15.8 m) long and weighed about 12 tons (11 tonnes).

CHUANJIESAURUS

Chuanjiesaurus was one of the largest early **sauropods**. It was named after the village of Chuanjie in China, Asia, where its fossils were discovered. It was similar in shape to *Mamenchisaurus*. It had a very long neck that it used to reach vegetation in places where its large body could not go such as thick forests or boggy marshland.

Chuanjiesaurus lived between **172–162 million years ago**. Fossil remains have been found in China, Asia. It grew to 82 feet (25 m) long and weighed 4 tons (3.6 tonnes).

DATOUSAURUS

Datousaurus means "big-head lizard" because its head was unusually large for a **sauropod**. It was a medium-sized **sauropod** that probably shared its habitat with *Shunosaurus*. With increasing competition for food, the *Datousaurus* evolved with more elongated vertebrae so it could reach higher vegetation and would not have to compete for the same food. *Datousaurus* had very robust teeth, which suggests that it fed on tough, twiggy material.

Datousaurus lived **170 million years ago**. Fossil remains were found in China, Asia. It grew to a length of 50 feet (15.2 m), with an estimated weight of about 9 tons (8 tonnes).

EUSTREPTOSPONDYLUS

Eustreptospondylus means "well-curved vertebra." It was a large carnivorous **theropod** that roamed the shores of islands that are now part of southern England, Europe. It was a bipedal dinosaur with powerful hind legs and small, short arms. Its large skull had an enormous mouth with hundreds of blade-like teeth. It might have been able to swim from island to island in its search for prey. The first specimen found was one of the world's most complete **theropod** specimens.

Eustreptospondylus lived **165 million years ago**. Its fossil remains were found in England, Europe. It grew to sizes of 30 feet (9 m) long and weighed almost 1 ton (0.9 tonnes).

GASOSAURUS

Gasosaurus means "gas lizard" after a gasoline company that found it while constructing a factory. *Gasosaurus* was a medium-sized carnivorous **theropod** with strong arms, powerful legs and a stiff tail. Its skull has never been found, but it is believed to be related to the **allosaurs** and is similar to *Monolophosaurus* (see page 20).

Gasosaurus lived **170–165 million years ago**. Its fossil remains were found in China, Asia. It grew to a length of 13 feet (4 m) and its weight is estimated at between 330 and 880 pounds (150–400 kg).

HUAYANGOSAURUS

Huayangosaurus' name comes from the area where it was found in China, Asia, meaning "Huayang lizard." It was a relatively small primitive **stegosaur**, a quadrupedal herbivore. Its back plates were more like spikes, and spines protruded outward from its shoulders. Like all **stegosaurs** its tail ended with two pairs of sharp spikes, known as the thagomizer. It swung its tail at any predator that got too close and could cause serious injury if it connected with an attacker.

Huayangosaurus lived **165 million years ago**. Fossil remains were found in the Sichuan (Huayang) Province of China, Asia. It grew to 14.8 feet (4.5 m) long and weighed approximately 1.1 tons (1 tonne).

JOBARIA

Jobaria was named after a mythical giant creature, local to Niger, Africa, called "Jobar." The dinosaur was mistakenly thought to be this creature when it was first discovered. *Jobaria* was in fact a large herbivorous **sauropod**. It was quite tall with long legs. Its center of gravity was toward its rear legs. This allowed it to rear up to reach higher vegetation. It shared its habitat with *Afrovenator*, a lightweight, meat-eating **theropod**, which might have preyed on its juveniles.

Jobaria lived between **168–157 million years ago**. Fossil remains were found in Niger, Africa. It grew to 60 feet (18.3 m) long and weighed in the region of 24.7 tons (22.4 tonnes).

LAPPARENTOSAURUS

Lapparentosaurus means "Lapparent's lizard" and is named after a French paleontologist. It was a fairly large herbivorous **sauropod**, related to *Brachiosaurus*. Its hind legs were smaller than its front legs, giving it a sloped back. Its long neck allowed it to browse for vegetation high up in the tops of trees. It might even have been able to rear up on its back legs to reach the highest branches.

Lapparentosaurus lived **169–165 million years ago**. Fossil remains were found in Madagascar, Africa. It grew to between 40 and 50 feet (12.2–15.2 m) in length and weighed around 5.5 to 11 tons (5–10 tonnes).

LEXOVISAURUS

Lexovisaurus' name comes from a tribe of celts who lived in the area where the original fossils were found. The literal meaning is "Lexovii lizard." It was a large **stegosaur**, and was one of the first fossils of a dinosaur from the Jurassic period ever found in Europe. Like all **stegosaurs** it walked on four legs and ate vegetation at low to medium height. It had a combination of small plates and large spines running down its back. Two large spikes protruded from the shoulders.

Lexovisaurus lived **164 million years ago**. Its fossil remains were found in England, Europe. It could grow to between 16.5 and 19.7 feet (5–6 m) in length and weighed around 5.5 tons (5 tonnes).

MEGALOSAURUS

Megalosaurus, meaning "great lizard," was a large, meat-eating **theropod**. It was one of the earliest dinosaur fossils to be discovered. It was the top predator of its time and hunted plant-eating dinosaurs. Its jaws were lined with long, dagger-like teeth that were ideal for slicing through the flesh of its prey.

Megalosaurus lived **170–155 million years ago**. Fossil remains have been found in England, Europe. It grew up to 29.5 feet (9 m) long and weighed around 1.1 tons (1 tonne).

MONOLOPHOSAURUS

Monolophosaurus means "single-crested lizard," named after the single bony crest that extends from the dinosaur's brow ridge down to the tip of its snout! The crest may have been used to amplify sounds intended to attract mates. It was a large carnivorous **theropod** that hunted **stegosaurs** and **sauropods**. It lived in an area known to be very wet, with coastal regions and lakes.

Monolophosaurus lived about **170 million years ago**. Fossil remains were found in northwest China, Asia. It grew to 16.5 feet (5 m) long and weighed in the region of 1,050 pounds (476 kg).

OMEISAURUS

Omeisaurus, named "Omei lizard," was named after a sacred mountain in China where its fossils were found. *Omeisaurus* was a very large herbivorous **sauropod**. It walked on four powerful, column-like legs, and used its exceptionally long neck to browse for vegetation in the tops of trees. Measuring an incredible 30 feet (9.1 m) long, its neck was longer than any other dinosaur's, except for *Mamenchisaurus*! Like many **sauropods**, fully grown it was relatively safe from predators. Only the very largest of the **theropods**, such as *Yangchuanosaurus*, would be a threat.

Omeisaurus lived about **169–160 million years ago**. Fossil remains were found in the Sichuan Province of China, Asia. It grew to a length of 66 feet (20.2 m) and weighed up to 10.8 tons (9.8 tonnes).

PATAGOSAURUS

Patagosaurus was discovered in South America and is named after the area where it was found — "Patagonia lizard." It was a large **sauropod** for its era, and is well-known since many fossils have been found. It is a very primitive **sauropod** that did not grow to the gigantic size of *Argentinosaurus*. It is often seen as a close relative of the European **sauropod** *Cetiosaurus* (see page 10). It used its long neck to browse for mid to high vegetation, and its whip-like tail to protect it from predators.

Patagosaurus lived **165 million years ago**. Its fossil remains were found in Argentina, South America. It grew to 49 feet (15 m) long and weighed around 10.5 tons (9.4 tonnes).

POEKILOPLEURON

Poekilopleuron means "varied ribs," after a perfect set of fossilized ribs were found. It was a large carnivorous **theropod**. Its fossils were found in the late 19th century, but they were destroyed during a battle in World War II. Today paleontologists only have the plaster casts to work from. The **theropod** was a powerful hunter. It stalked the woodland habitats of Western Europe, using its powerful jaws and arms to catch its prey.

Poekilopleuron lived **170–165 million year ago**. Fossil remains were found in France, Europe. It grew to 29.5 feet (9 m) long and weighed around 1.1 tons (1 tonne).

PROCERATOSAURUS

Proceratosaurus means "before ceratosaurs" and is named after the horn-like crest on its snout that resembles *Ceratosaurus'*. It was a medium-sized **theropod** with a very graceful and agile build. It was a predatory and speedy hunter, but since it was not the largest predator of its area, it would have needed its speed, too, to flee from larger **theropods** such as *Eustreptospondylus* (see page 13).

Proceratosaurus lived between **170–164 million years ago**. Its fossils remains were found in England, Europe. It grew to 13.6 feet (4.1 m) long and weighed about 500 pounds (227 kg).

SHUNOSAURUS

Meaning "Shu lizard," *Shunosaurus* was named after where it was found — Shu is the ancient name for the Sichuan province in China, Asia. *Shunosaurus* was a herbivorous **sauropod**. It had a small neck for a **sauropod**, and its long tail ended, unusually, in a spiked club. This was used to thwack any predators that dared to get too close.

Shunosaurus lived about **170 million years ago**. Fossil remains have been found in China, Asia. It grew to 31 feet (9.5 m) long and weighed around 3.3 tons (3 tonnes).

SINRAPTOR

Sinraptor, meaning "Chinese thief," was a medium-sized carnivorous **theropod**, related to dinosaurs like *Giganotosaurus*. Like most **theropods** it had powerful jaws, and strong back legs to run down its prey. It had a long, stiff tail that counterbalanced its large skull. It fed on juvenile **sauropods** and smaller dinosaurs such as *Epidexipteryx*.

Sinraptor lived between **170–145 million years ago**. Its fossil remains were found in China, Asia. It grew up to 25 feet (7.6 m) long and weighed about 1.1 tons (1 tonne).

SPINOPHOROSAURUS

Spinophorosaurus, meaning "spine-bearing lizard," was an unusual **sauropod** in that it had spikes at the end of its tail. Known as thagomizers, these tail spikes were similar to the thagomizers of some **stegosaur** dinosaurs such as *Stegosaurus* and *Huayangosaurus* (see page 15). Scientists think they were used as a defensive weapon against predators.

Spinophorosaurus lived around **170 million years ago.** Fossil remains have been found in Niger, Africa. It grew up to 46 feet (14 m) long and weighed around 9.9 tons (9 tonnes).

XIAOSAURUS

Xiaosaurus means "small lizard," although it was not particularly small. *Xiaosaurus* was an **ornithischian** herbivore. Like all **ornithopods** it was a fast grazer, preferring to run around at high speeds on two legs, using its stiff tail as a balance for making tight turns. It had five-fingered hands and four-toed feet, with a small head and large eyes. It might have been the ancestor of *Hypsilophodon*.

Xiaosaurus lived between **170–160 million years ago**. Its fossil remains were found in China, Asia. It grew to about 5 feet (1.5 m) long and weighed around 100 pounds (45.4 kg).

YANDUSAURUS

Yandusaurus is named after the area where it was found in China, Asia. It was a fast-paced herbivorous, bipedal, early **ornithopod**. It had four toes on each foot and five fingers on each hand. It had large eyes to keep a look out for predators and used its speed and agility to evade them. The first fossil was found on a building site. Although its fossils had been heavily damaged by building machines paleontologists were still able to recover enough to discover it was a brand-new species.

Yandusaurus lived **169–163 million years ago**. Its fossil remains were found in the Sichuan province of China, Asia. It grew up to an estimated 11.4 feet (3.5 m) long and weighed a maximum of 308 pounds (140 kg).

YUANMOUSAURUS

Yuanmousaurus was found in Yuanmou County in China, Asia. Its name means "Yuanmou lizard." It was a large **sauropod** by Jurassic standards, with a long neck used to browse for the juiciest of vegetation at the tops of trees! *Yuanmousaurus* had many similarities with *Mamenchisaurus*, including its long neck and tail. Its large, pillar-like legs had a thumb spike that may have been used as a defense against predators or to help cling on to tree trunks as it reared up on its back legs.

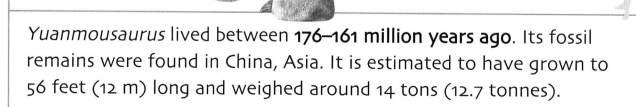

Yuanmousaurus lived between **176–161 million years ago**. Its fossil remains were found in China, Asia. It is estimated to have grown to 56 feet (12 m) long and weighed around 14 tons (12.7 tonnes).

GLOSSARY

allosaur
A member of a group of large bipedal carnivorous dinosaurs common in North America.

cetiosaur
A member of a family of sauropods.

megalosaur
A group of fairly primitive, stiff-tailed, carnivorous theropod dinosaurs, with razor-sharp teeth and three claws on each hand. This group included *Megalosaurus*, and *Torvosaurus*.

ornithischia
A group of dinosaurs characterized by their "bird-hips" and beaks.

ornithopod
A group of "bird-hipped" dinosaurs characterized by being fast-paced grazers, becoming one of the most successful herbivore groups.

plesiosaur
A group of marine reptiles that thrived in the Jurassic and Cretaceous periods, so successful that they had a worldwide oceanic distribution.

pliosaur
A member of the plesiosaurs, they were large marine reptiles with elongated heads, hundreds of teeth, short necks and large rear flippers.

pterosaur
Flying reptile — includes Pterodactylus.

sauropod
A group of large, four-legged, herbivorous dinosaurs with long necks and long tails. This group included the well-known *Brachiosaurus*, *Diplodocus* and *Apatosaurus*.

stegosaur
A member of a group of quadrupedal herbivores, characterized by their bony plates and, occasionally, a thagomizer.

theropod
The large group of lizard-hipped dinosaurs that walked on two legs and included most of the giant carnivores such as *Tyrannosaurus*.

INDEX